To Imogen. And to all mothers, great artists,
creating beauty out of chaos. —A.N.

For Clay. —L.C.

Thank you to the Partridge family: Elizabeth, Meg and Rondal.
I couldn't have made this book without you.

IMOGEN

The Mother of Modernism and Three Boys

by Amy Novesky

illustrated by Lisa Congdon

Imogen was named after a princess in a Shakespeare play, but she didn't expect life to be smooth and easy and beautiful.

Her family didn't have much, and life was hard atop the wild hill they called home. Her mother took care of Imogen and her five siblings. Her father taught her to read and to draw. On Sundays, Imogen helped him pull taffy instead of going to church.

When Imogen was a teenager, she declared she wanted to be a photographer. Her father wondered why she'd choose such a messy profession. But he built her a darkroom in the woodshed, lit by a single candle in a red box.

Imogen worked her way through school. She studied chemistry and botany. She read poetry. She was the only one in her family to graduate from a university. It was the beginning of the twentieth century.

With only a few dollars in her pocket, she opened a portrait studio in the city. She gave flowers to her subjects and told them to think about the nicest thing they knew.

With its heavy glass plates, cumbersome equipment and chemicals for developing film, photography was indeed a messy profession. Imogen loved it.

Then she fell in love with an etcher named Roi who wrote
her long letters from Paris. They had a small wedding and
spent hours outdoors make-believing scenes from fairytales.
Imogen took photographs that looked like paintings.

Soon, Imogen and Roi had a baby boy named Gryffyd, and nearly two years later, two more—the twins, Rondal and Padraic. Suddenly Imogen had her hands full taking care of her sons. There was barely enough money for film after food was bought, and three hungry boys to cook for at dawn and dusk, when the light was just right.

Imogen wanted to take pictures. But she couldn't leave the house.

And so she focused on her family.

She built a darkroom at home and turned the garden into a wonderland for her boys and a workshop for herself.

She cultivated agave and aloe, flax and hyacinth, banana plant, Calla lilies, magnolias and morning glories.

While she worked, her boys played, and Imogen photographed them.

CLICK. The twins picking foxglove
buds. Her older son's wonder at a handful of
nasturtiums.

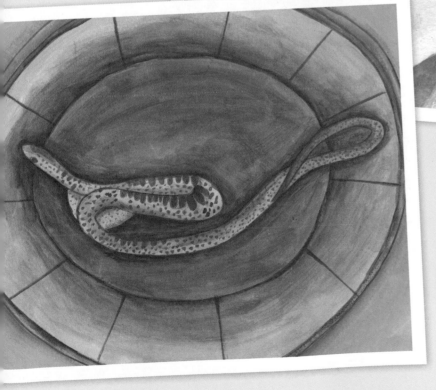

CLICK. One boy holding
a mouse, another a bird. A
snake in a bucket. They didn't
have an ordinary pet.

CLICK. Freckled ears and feathered headdresses.

Glowing birthday cakes. Her three growing boys.

She photographed her bespectacled father.
Her mother with a crown of silver spoons.

Imogen found a little beauty in everything.

And for one hour every afternoon, while the boys napped, Imogen focused on her flowers, including a common magnolia blossom she shot close up.

When one mischievous twin interrupted, Imogen sent
him out into the sun with her proof sheets until they were
developed.

She set up an apple box for him to stand on to pluck prints
out of the chemical baths when they were done.

After a day's work, when the light was just right, and the house was alight with three hungry boys, Imogen cooked for them. She didn't expect life to be smooth and easy and beautiful.

But sometimes it was.

AUTHOR'S NOTE

"You can't expect things to be smooth and easy and beautiful. You just have to work, find your way out, and do anything you can yourself."

—Imogen Cunningham

"Self-Portrait with My Children, early 1920s"   © IMOGEN CUNNINGHAM TRUST 2012

Imogen Cunningham was one of the finest photographers of the twentieth century, and she was a devoted mother. One hand in the dishpan, the other in the darkroom, she was called "the mother of modernism and three boys."

At the turn of the century, there weren't many women photographers. Women were expected to focus on children and the home, not the higher arts. Imogen focused on her children and her home—she photographed them. Working from home allowed Imogen to be with her family, and photographing them led Imogen to focus on the plants and flowers—most notably her signature magnolia blossoms—for which she is best known.

As a child, Imogen lived on Queen Anne Hill in Seattle. But she spent most of her life in the Bay Area with her husband, Roi, and their sons, Gryffyd, Rondal and Padraic. Then she lived in a little white cottage on Green Street in San Francisco. When she wasn't taking photographs, she tended her beloved garden, which grew with bougainvillea, Mexican mock orange, a rare black begonia, and a geranium from Virginia Woolf's garden.

November 12th is Imogen Cunningham Day in the city that loved her.

To learn more about Imogen Cunningham, please see:
· *Mother's Days*, a book by Little Bear Press
· *Portrait of Imogen*, a film by Meg Partridge
· www.ImogenCunningham.com